DEPARTMENT OF THE NAVY
HEADQUARTERS UNITED STATES MARINE CORPS
3000 MARINE CORPS PENTAGON
WASHINGTON, DC 20350-3000

I0430279

MARINE CORPS CYBERSECURITY PROGRAM (MCCSP)

DEPARTMENT OF THE NAVY
HEADQUARTERS UNITED STATES MARINE CORPS
3000 MARINE CORPS PENTAGON
WASHINGTON, DC 20350-3000

MCO 5239.2A
C4
July 18 2012

MARINE CORPS ORDER 5239.2A

From: Commandant of the Marine Corps
To: Distribution List

Subj: MARINE CORPS CYBERSECURITY PROGRAM (MCCSP)

Ref: (a) DoD Instruction 8500.2, "Information Assurance
           Implementation," February 6, 2003
       (b) DoD Instruction 8510.01, "DOD Information Assurance
           Certification and Accreditation Process (DIACAP),"
           November 28, 2007
       (c) DoD Directive 8500.01E, "Information Assurance (IA),"
           October 24, 2002
       (d) SECNAVINST 5239.3B, "DON Information Assurance
           Policy," June 17, 2009
       (e) SECNAV M-5239.1, "DON Information Assurance Program
           Information Assurance Manual," November 2005
       (f) DON DIACAP Handbook, DON DOD Information Assurance
           Certification and Accreditation Process (DIACAP)
           Handbook, Ver. 1.0 of July 15, 2008
       (g) MCO 5400.52 "DON Deputy Chief Information Officer
           Marine Corps Roles and Responsibilities", January
           2010
       (h) DoD Instruction 8580.1, "Information Assurance (IA)
           in the Defense Acquisition System," July 9, 2004
       (i) DoD Instruction 5220.22, "National Industrial
           Security Program (NISP)," March 18, 2011
       (j) DoD Instruction 8581.1, "Information Assurance (IA)
           Policy for Space Systems Used by the Department of
           Defense," June 8, 2010
       (k) CJCSI 6211.02D, "Defense Information System Network
           (DISN) Responsibilities," January 24, 2012
       (l) CJCSI 6212.01E, "Interoperability and Supportability
           of Information Technology and National Security
           Systems," December 15, 2008

DISTRIBUTION STATEMENT A: Approved for public release;
distribution is unlimited.

(m) SECNAVINST 5400.15C, "DON Research and Development, Acquisition, Associated Life-Cycle Management, and Logistics Responsibilities and Accountability," September 13, 2007

(n) CJCSI 3170.01G, "Joint Capabilities Integration and Development System," March 1, 2009

(o) DoD 5000.2-R, "Mandatory Procedures for Major Defense Acquisition Programs (MDAPS) and Major Automated Information System (MAIS) Acquisition Programs," April 5, 2002

(p) "Interim Defense Acquisition Guidebook," July 7, 2009

(q) DoD Directive 5000.01, "The Defense Acquisition System," May 12, 2003

(r) DEPSECDEF Memorandum, "The Definition of Cyberspace," May 12, 2008 (NOTAL)

(s) DoD Instruction O-8530.2, "Support to Computer Network Defense (CND)," November 3, 2008

(t) DoD Directive 5205.02-M, "DOD Operations Security (OPSEC) Program," March 6, 2006

(u) DoD Manual O-8530.1-M, "Department of Defense Computer Network Defense (CND) Service Provider Certification and Accreditation Program," December 17, 2003 (NOTAL)

(v) CJCS Memorandum, "Definition of Cyberspace Operations," November 10, 2008 (NOTAL)

(w) CJCSI 6510.01F, "Information Assurance (IA) and Support to Computer Network Defense (CND)," February 9, 2011

(x) DoD Directive 8570.01, "Information Assurance (IA) Training, Certification, and Workforce Management," April 23, 2007

(y) SECNAVINST 5239.19, "DON Computer Network Incident Response and Reporting Requirements," March 18, 2008

(z) DoD Instruction 5230.29, "Security and Policy Review of DOD Information for Public Release," January 8, 2009

(aa) SECNAVINST 5211.5E, "DON Privacy Program," December 28, 2005

(ab) MCO 3070.2

(ac) ALNAV 070/07 "DON PII Annual Training Policy," October 4, 2007

(ad) SECNAVINST 3030.4C, "DON Continuity of Operations Program," July 22, 2009 (ae) DOD 8570.01-M, "Information Assurance Workforce Improvement Program," December 19, 2005

(af) DoD 5500.7-R, "Joint Ethics Regulations," August 1, 1993

(ag) DoD Directive 1344.10, "Political Activities by Members of the Armed Forces," February 19, 2008

(ah) SECNAV M-5210.1, "DON Records Management Program Records Management Manual," November 2007

(ai) HQMC C4 MCIENT Strategy, October 2011

(aj) CJCSM 6510.01A: "Information Assurance and Computer Network Defense Volume 1 (Incident Handling Program)", June 24, 2009

(ak) DoD Instruction 8520.03, "Identity Authentication for Information Systems", May 13, 2011

(al) NIST Special Publication 800-37, Revision 1, February, 2010

(am) SECNAV M-5210.1

Encl: (1) Definitions
       (2) Acronyms

1. <u>Situation</u>

   a. Our adversaries continue to become more technically and tactically sophisticated. They are utilizing low-cost attack tools making them a formidable and dangerous threat. Others are far more sophisticated with financial backing and nation state support. The implementation and adherence to policies and guidelines that support strong protection, detection, response, restoration, remediation, and mitigation activities are key to achieving and maintaining dominance on the cyber battlefield. It is imperative to implement timely, cost-effective, and proactive cybersecurity practices to increase the Marine Corps' ability to identify and mitigate vulnerabilities and threats before exploitation can occur.

   b. The Marine Corps Cybersecurity Program (MCCSP) is an enterprise-wide approach to protect United States Marine Corps critical information and intelligence from internal and external threats and attacks to ensure our Warfighters achieve and maintain information dominance during all phases of the full spectrum of military operations. The MCCSP establishes a unified approach to ensure the confidentiality, integrity, and availability of unclassified, sensitive, and classified information received, stored, processed, displayed, or transmitted by Marine Corps information systems; consolidates and focuses Marine Corps efforts in securing the information, including its associated systems and resources; increases the level of trust of this information and the originating source; and provides identity assurance to all users accessing the Marine Corps Enterprise Network (MCEN).

    c. Operationally, failure to implement the proactive or corrective cybersecurity measures identified in this Order may result in critical information loss, capture, corruption, or lack of timely access leading to potential mission non-accomplishment. Administratively, it may prevent system or enclave accreditation, installation, or operation. Cybersecurity and/or network personnel may block access to information systems that have been determined to adhere to poor cybersecurity practices or fail to implement identified corrective measures. Additionally, systems on the MCEN processing intelligence information are required to adhere to the provisions of this Order.

    d. The Marine Corps Sensitive Compartmented Information (SCI) networks and systems are protected under the Marine Corps Director of Intelligence (DIRINT) SCI Enterprise Office (SEO). The SEO provides an enterprise-wide approach to protect Marine Corps critical SCI residing within Marine Corps Intelligence Surveillance and Reconnaissance Enterprise (MCISR-E) from intended or unintended malicious attacks from internal and external threats. The SEO Cybersecurity responsibilities are governed by policies and directives from the Office of the Director of National Intelligence (ODNI), Defense Intelligence Agency (DIA) and the National Security Agency (NSA).

2. <u>Cancellation</u>. MCO 5239.2

3. <u>Mission</u>. This Order provides the policy, procedures, and standards implementation guidance applicable to the MCEN. An ANNEX providing the policy, procedures, and standards implementation guidance for Marine Corps SCI Networks will be published 180 days from the issuance of this Order. It delineates all organizational actions required to ensure the security of voice communication and digital information in all of its forms, and the security of the systems and networks where information is stored, accessed, processed, and transmitted. This includes precautions taken to guard against cyber attack in order to provide an end-to-end secure networking capability to protect and deliver secure information at the right time, to the

right place, and in a useable format, thereby allowing commanders to exercise freedom of command and control. The base Order applies to the MCEN.

4. Execution

    a. Commander's Intent and Concept of Operations

        (1) Commander's Intent. MCCSP mission success will be accomplished by employing a comprehensive cybersecurity program designed to protect and defend the MCEN and the information residing on the MCEN to ultimately support the commander's information needs. New technologies such as web services and portals are emerging in support of developmental, training, testing, exercise, and operational deployments. The MCCSP, a comprehensive framework for security governance and controls over information resources, will facilitate the rapid assimilation of these new technologies and information processing methodologies, executed by a professional cyber workforce, in a flexible, proactive manner and will continue to improve efforts to effectively manage and monitor network and system activities. The Marine Corps must employ a cybersecurity capability that supports a robust, enterprise-wide, "best network security practices", and posture to improve Cyber-Security implementation and situational awareness across the MCEN. The MCCSP will incorporate proactive protection, detection, reaction, disaster recovery, and restoration capabilities to include the detection of, reporting on, and countermeasures against unauthorized activities. Concurrently, the effectiveness of cybersecurity programs, policies, and procedures will be reviewed by means of established procedures.

        (2) Concept of Operations. The Marine Corps will adopt an information system "life-cycle management" approach in applying uniform standards for the protection of Marine Corps Information Technology (IT) resources that display, transact, transmit, or receive information. The Marine Corps will iteratively assess threats, vulnerabilities, risks, and a spectrum of cybersecurity practices to identify, document, and implement appropriate countermeasures to effectively mitigate risks to an acceptable operational level.

(3) <u>Tasks</u>

 (a) <u>Director, Command, Control, Communications, and Computers (C4)/Chief Information Officer (CIO) of the Marine Corps</u> shall:

 <u>1</u>. Exercise oversight authority and CIO governance for all matters and programs regarding the MCCSP and be responsible directly to the CMC for cybersecurity policies and programs enacted throughout the Marine Corps (excluding (SCI) networks).

 <u>2</u>. Execute the duties as the Marine Corps Authorizing Official (AO) (excluding SCI systems) for the MCEN in accordance with references (a) through (f).

 <u>3</u>. Designate a Marine Corps Senior Information Assurance Official (SIAO) for the MCEN and maintain a Cross Domain Solutions (CDS) Office.

 <u>4</u>. Create, promulgate, inspect, validate, oversee, and execute the MCCSP.

 <u>5</u>. Develop, issue, and maintain Marine Corps cybersecurity policies and procedures to implement the MCCSP and serve as the focal point for Marine Corps Cybersecurity programs and funding for the MCEN.

 <u>6</u>. Chair the Cybersecurity Steering Group (CSSG), chartered under the C4 Operational Advisory Group (C4 OAG), responsible to coordinate and standardize cybersecurity standards and practices implemented throughout the MCEN.

 <u>7</u>. Coordinate with the Director of Intelligence (DIRINT) to ensure SEO representation in the cybersecurity working groups, the CDS Office, and the CSSG to adequately represent SCI networks.

 <u>8</u>. Standardize Marine Corps' cybersecurity policies, procedures, directives, and guidance to adhere to applicable Federal, Department of Defense (DoD), Department of the Navy (DON), and Marine Corps cybersecurity directives.

 <u>9</u>. Ensure Marine Corps cybersecurity requirements are

developed, validated, and forwarded for inclusion in appropriate Federal, DoD, and DON cybersecurity directives.

    10. Ensure Marine Corps representation to DoD, Joint, and DON cybersecurity panels and working groups.

    11. Establish and maintain a standardized Marine Corps Security, Test, and Evaluation (ST&E) methodology, Certification and Accreditation (C&A) Program, and security requirements as part of the Marine Corps C&A Process (MCCAP).

    12. Establish and maintain a Marine Corps Cyber Assessment Team (MCCAT) in order to identify vulnerabilities in order to reduce the overall risk to the MCEN in a collaborated effort.

    13. Document, develop, coordinate, advocate, and prioritize Marine Corps cybersecurity resource requirements in the planning, programming, budgeting and execution process.

    14. Coordinate with the Naval Communications Security (COMSEC) Management Service (NCMS) for policy development and dissemination, support, tactics, techniques, and procedures (TTPs) for the design, implementation, and operation of the Key Management Infrastructure (KMI) and systems to support Marine Corps cryptographic requirements.

    15. Provide program oversight for Marine Corps implementation of the KMI and funding aspects of the Electronic Key Management System (EKMS) and provide cybersecurity guidance to Marine Corps elements to identify and incorporate requirements consistent with the KMI in project development.

    16. Represent the Marine Corps as a voting member on the Key Management Executive Committee (KMEC) and Joint Key Management Infrastructure Working Group (JKMIWG).

    17. Provide program oversight for the Marine Corps implementation of the Public Key Infrastructure (PKI) as directed by DoD.

    18. Prepare the annual Marine Corps Information Assurance (IA) Readiness Report and Marine Corps input to the annual DON IA Report to include Federal Information Systems Management Act (FISMA) data collection and reporting in

accordance with reference (a) and reporting to DoD IT Portfolio Repository - Department of the Navy (DITPR-DON).

19. Manage the Inspector General of the Marine Corps (IGMC) Functional Area Checklist (405) "Information System Management" program and provide technical and operational assistance to the Naval Audit Service (NAS) and the Marine Corps Inspector General in audits and reviews of Marine Corps information systems.

20. Evaluate technological trends in cybersecurity and sponsor research activities to identify, define, and integrate technological advancements into the Marine Corps capability sets of cybersecurity.

21. Represent the Marine Corps on the Committee on National Security Systems (CNSS) and the Subcommittees for Telecommunications Security (STS) and Information System Security (SISS).

22. Represent the Marine Corps on the Defense/IA Security Accreditation Working Group (DSAWG) and share presented material with Marine Forces Cyberspace Command (MARFORCYBER).

23. Represent the Marine Corps on the DoD Enterprise-wide IA and CND Solutions Steering Group (ESSG).

24. Represent the Marine Corps on the DoD IA Steering Group (IASG).

25. Provide policy, guidance, and oversight to employ the National Institute of Standards and Technology (NIST) approved cryptography standards to protect unclassified and sensitive information.

26. Provide oversight for Marine Corps Web Risk Assessment Cell (MWRAC) cybersecurity and support OPSEC programs and initiatives.

27. Coordinate with Commanding General, Training and Education Command (TECOM) to ensure cybersecurity training requirements are identified, developed, and provided to all military members, government civilians, and contract personnel who have access to any portion of the DoD Global Information Grid (GIG) and the MCEN.

28. Coordinate with Commander, Marine Corps Systems Command (MARCORSYSCOM) and Deputy Commandant, Combat Development and Integration (CD&I) to validate Marine Corps COMSEC and cybersecurity capabilities to ensure they are fully defined and resourced during the development of the DON Program Objective Memorandum (POM).

29. Evaluate IT procurement requests (ITPRs) within the ITPR Review and Approval System (ITPRAS) for compliance with cybersecurity policies and Marine Corps Enterprise Network (MCEN) authorized configuration requirements prior to approval.

30. Provide service voting member representation to the Committee for National Security Systems.

(b) Deputy Commandant for Combat Development and Integration (CD & I) shall:

1. Ensure cybersecurity requirements are incorporated into applicable Joint Capabilities Integration and Development System (JCIDS) and other capabilities documents (e.g., Urgent Universal Needs Statement (UUNS)) even if the IT is only a subcomponent of the entire system. Ensure that the Doctrine, Organization, Training, Materiel, Leadership and Education, Personnel, Facilities (DOTMLPF) process accounts for Cybersecurity requirements.

2. Coordinate with the Commanding General MARFORCYBER, Commander, Marine Corps Systems Command (MARCORSYSCOM) and the Director, HQMC C4 for the integration of enterprise level cybersecurity interoperability requirements.

3. Coordinate with the SEO for integration of SCI level systems, capabilities, requirements and interoperability.

(c) Commanding General, MARFORCYBER shall:

1. Coordinate the defense of Marine Corps computer systems and networks on the MCEN as directed by the United States Cyber Command (USCYBERCOM).

     2.   Coordinate Cyber Conditions (CYBERCON) in response to Offensive Cyber Operations (OCO) and report the Marine Corps CYBERCON status to USCYBERCOM.

     3.   In coordination with the Marine Corps Network Operations and Security Center (MCNOSC), aggregate Intrusion Detection/Prevention Systems (IDS/IPS) data and key network device logs and provide incident trend and correlation analysis of network traffic across the MCEN and make this information available to organizations with a valid need to know.

     4.   Integrate Defensive Cyber Operations (DCO), Operations Security (OPSEC), and CYBERCON activities into cyber and information operations (IO) in accordance with references (c), (k), (l), and (r) through (v) in coordination with the Deputy Commandant for Plans, Programs, and Operations (DC PP&O).

     5.   Develop and maintain a Marine Corps Computer Network Defense (CND) vulnerability and threat database for situational awareness monitoring, reporting, event correlation, and trend analysis.

     6.   Develop tactics, techniques, and procedures (TTPs) for a threat warning and notification process.

     7.   Develop procedures to issue CND lessons learned identified from incidents, intrusions, forensic analyses, or other technical processes in coordination with HQMC C4 to higher, adjacent, and supporting cybersecurity organizations.

     8.   Coordinate and collaborate with HQMC C4, HQMC Intelligence (HQMC I), and the MARFORs, to conduct, receive and/or provide technical analyses and studies concerning cyber threats in order to support cybersecurity decision makers.

     9.   Coordinate with Intel Department to provide intelligence support to cybersecurity decision makers.

     10.   Coordinate with C4 and MCNOSC to execute Cyber Red Team Operations against MCEN targets through effective employment of remote network operations, wireless exploitation, and close access to validate and test the MCEN security posture.

(d) <u>Director, Intelligence shall</u>:

<u>1</u>. As the Marine Corps principal for intelligence, special access, and SCI programs to include Marine Corps SCI Facilities (SCIFs), networks and systems, adhere to the cybersecurity directives, policies, and guidance from ODNI, DIA, and NSA.

<u>2</u>. Exercise oversight authority for all SCI matters and programs regarding the MCCSP and be responsible directly to the Commandant of the Marine Corps (CMC) for SCI cybersecurity policies and programs enacted throughout the Marine Corps.

<u>3</u>. The DIRINT will publish an ANNEX 180 days from the issuance of this Order, in coordination with the Director C4, providing the policy, procedures, standards and implementation guidance for Marine Corps SCI Networks.

<u>4</u>. Provide HQMC C4 and the MARFORs with service-level intelligence support of foreign cyber intelligence threats.

(e) <u>Commander, Marine Corps Systems Command shall</u>:

<u>1</u>. Execute Technical Authority responsibilities as delegated to MARCORSYSCOM under reference (m) in the MCCSP execution for Program of Record (POR)/Centrally Managed Programs.

<u>2</u>. Acquire and field validated materiel solutions in support of defined capability requirements compliant with DoD, DON, and Marine Corps cybersecurity policy and guidance applicable to the particular materiel solutions. The information systems and products will be developed and supported per this Order.

<u>3</u>. Embed cybersecurity engineering and capabilities in all information systems as early as possible in the acquisition process.

<u>4</u>. Integrate cybersecurity, identity management, COMSEC, and TEMPEST into the entire system life. This will ensure that the use of market-driven/industry-developed (MDID), commercial-off-the-shelf (COTS), government-off-the-shelf (GOTS), or other products that are consistent and tested will comply

with cybersecurity requirements and do not introduce unacceptable levels of risk.

  <u>5</u>. Ensure cybersecurity requirements are engineered and incorporated in the earliest phases of the system acquisition, contracting, and development life cycles in accordance with reference (n).

  <u>6</u>. Ensure program managers acquire systems in accordance with the provisions of this Order to establish timely, cost-effective, and proactive cybersecurity capabilities. Included in this effort are identity management and cybersecurity measures which are designed to identify vulnerabilities and threats.

  <u>7</u>. Ensure funding requirements are identified to have a DIACAP package submitted to HQMC C4, or SEO for SCI Systems, for approval. Provide a copy of the final system security documentation via the directed automated C&A tool for accreditation approval before operational deployment of the system in accordance with references (a) through (g) and (r). For UUNS or officially designated urgent requirements, coordinate with the AO no less than 90 days prior to operational deployment to ensure an accreditation approval can be completed within 30 days.

  <u>8</u>. Ensure the establishment Configuration Management Program (CMP) standards for programs of record across the MCEN. This includes ensuring integrated readiness reviews and compliance processes are in accordance with references (p) and (q).

  <u>9</u>. In coordination with DC CD&I, ensure appropriate manpower studies are conducted which reflect the addition of IT/cybersecurity personnel required to operate, administer, or maintain a new or expanded information system or network.

  <u>10</u>. Integrate cybersecurity engineering practices into pre-Milestone A through Milestone C activities and events as defined in references (d), (e), (g), (m), and (o).

  <u>11</u>. Assume responsibility for IT system life cycle management per reference (m).

    12. Perform acquisition and life cycle management of materiel in support of the acquisition IA strategy.

    13. Report to the HQMC C4 the percentage of Program Manager (PM)-programmed funding allocated to the MCCSP. The report will include current and planned MCEN cybersecurity investments and will be included in annual budgetary reports from HQMC C4 to DoD and DON.

    14. Adhere to cybersecurity standards for equipment per the DoD IT Standards (DITS) and the GIG cybersecurity architecture and maintain an inventory of information systems products, equipment, locations, and contact information.

    15. Adhere to USCYBERCOM and the MCNOSC patching requirements for all applications that support Programs of Record, by enacting timely Information Assurance Vulnerability Management (IAVM) compliance measures (e.g., testing, patching, compliance reporting, and program management). Incorporate them into life cycle management/sustainment procedures to ensure compliance actions are reported to the MCNOSC in accordance with USCYBERCOM task orders.

    16. Ensure cryptographic life cycle management is a consideration during the system design phase.

    17. Submit Marine Corps COMSEC POM requirements to support cybersecurity programs to HQMC C4 via DC CD&I, for validation and endorsement.

    18. Coordinate with the Marine Corps SCI Enterprise Office to ensure SCI systems and capabilities comply with SEO and IC enterprise initiatives.

    (f) Commanding General, Training and Education Command shall:

    1. Develop appropriate Military Occupational Specialty (MOS) Training and Readiness (T&R) events that integrate approved cybersecurity tools, doctrine, and TTPs into applicable programs of instruction to meet or exceed validated MCCSP requirements.

2. Incorporate cybersecurity training and education into all pertinent Marine Corps formal schools and distance learning classrooms from entry level training and continuing throughout a Marine's career to meet or exceed validated MCCSP requirements.

3. Coordinate with DC CD&I, HQMC C4, MARFORCYBERCOM to develop and maintain current and timely Marine Corps-wide cybersecurity training literature and training aids that leverage secure electronic distribution and remote access capabilities.

(g) Commanding Officer, Marine Corps Network Operations and Security Center (MCNOSC) shall:

1. Monitor Marine Corps Information Assurance Vulnerability Management (IAVM) program compliance and act as the Marine Corps' reporting agent and clearinghouse for Information Assurance Vulnerability Alert (IAVA) compliance and Information Assurance Vulnerability Bulletins (IAVBs).

2. Coordinate, as required, with Combatant Command (COCOM) and Marine Force Commanders to provide DCO support for deployed units.

3. Coordinate vulnerability assessments on the MCEN with the MCCAT to maintain the highest security posture.

4. Ensure Marine Corps websites are configured and maintained in compliance with prescribed Federal, DoD, and DON website administration policies and procedures.

5. Monitor network traffic between MCEN Point of Presence (POP) sites and the Defense Information Systems Network (DISN) and all network layers from external boundary to host level for intrusions, incidents, and anomalies, and provide appropriate impact assessments and response in real time and provide the information to cybersecurity organizations with a valid need to know.

6. Provide situational awareness to Regional NOSCs of threats, vulnerabilities, intrusions, incidents, and anomalies in area of responsibility traffic in order to enable effective reporting for regionalized impact assessments.

<u>7</u>. Report major impacts on Marine Corps operations; unusual network activities; violations of Federal, DoD, DON, and Marine Corps cybersecurity policies; and criminal acts conducted on Marine Corps IT resources through the appropriate chain of command or law enforcement/counter intelligence agencies.

<u>8</u>. Establish TTPs for the Marine Corps Computer Emergency Response Team (MARCERT) and Marine Forces (MARFOR) cybersecurity personnel in coordination with HQMC C4 as required for computer network operations (CNO).

<u>9</u>. Integrate computer incident response, impact assessment capabilities, cybersecurity, and CND service provider activities into network operations (NETOPS), network management, and information dissemination to ensure timely situational awareness across the MCEN.

<u>10</u>. Serve as the Marine Corps CND Service Provider for security incidents, intrusions, and violations, and in coordination with USCYBERCOMM, law enforcement (LE), Naval Criminal Investigative Service (NCIS), and counterintelligence (CI) agencies, develop and publish response guidelines, checklists, and procedures.

(h) <u>Commanding Generals and Commanding Officers</u> shall:

<u>1</u>. Be responsible for cybersecurity practices for all information systems and networks within their purview and to ensure systems' site C&A is in accordance with reference (f).

<u>2</u>. Appoint, in writing, an Information Systems Security Manager (ISSM) for the MCEN and another for the SCI network capabilities within the command. Ensure the ISSM receives applicable certifications in accordance with reference (ae) and can perform required duties. The ISSM functions as the Command focal point and principal advisor for all cybersecurity matters on behalf of the Commander. The ISSM reports to the Commander and implements the overall cybersecurity program within their area of responsibility.

<u>3</u>. Ensure a Information Systems Security Officer (ISSO) is designated, as appropriate, for each information

system and network in the organization. Ensure the ISSO receives applicable training in accordance with reference (x) to carry out their duties. The ISSO acts on behalf of the ISSM to ensure compliance with cybersecurity procedures at the operational site or facility.

<u>4</u>. Ensure all personnel performing privileged user functions that have cybersecurity impacts (e.g., system administrators, network administrators, and operators) receive initial basic cybersecurity and system specific training as well as annual, refresher, and follow-on cybersecurity training. Ensure that all personnel with privileged user capabilities are certified in accordance with reference (y).

<u>5</u>. Ensure cybersecurity awareness indoctrination and annual refresher training is conducted and documented down to the user level and is tailored to specific site requirements.

<u>6</u>. Ensure current cybersecurity standard operating procedures are available, used, and updated regularly for each IT resource.

<u>7</u>. Report as directed all security incidents (e.g., intrusions, malware, spillages, etc.) and incident suspicions to the MCNOSC or SEO for SCI systems, in accordance with the reference. Incident response, handling, and reporting requirements shall be conducted in accordance with reference (y).

<u>8</u>. Review certification documentation for systems under their purview, including Urgent Universal Needs Statements (UUNS), to evaluate and determine an acceptable level of risk and recommend accreditation accordingly. Ensure the proper Plan of Actions and Milestones (POA&Ms) are generated for documentation and monitoring purposes.

<u>9</u>. Ensure compliance with Federal, DoD, DON, and Marine Corps information systems and web site administration policies and implement content-approval procedures to ensure that no cybersecurity, OPSEC, or Personally Identifiable Information (PII) violations occur in accordance with references (a), (t), and (z) through (ac).

<u>10</u>. Develop a Disaster Recovery/Continuity of Operations Plan (DR/COOP) in accordance with references (a), (w),

and (ad) to ensure recovery and sustainment of information systems and services following an event, incident, or disaster.

11. Ensure the implementation of a privacy program in accordance with reference (aa) which provides guidance regarding the collection, safeguarding, maintenance, use, access, amendment, and dissemination of PII maintained by DOD, DON, and the Marine Corps in Privacy Act programs and systems of records.

12. Ensure the establishment and implementation of a Configuration Management Program (CMP), consistent with Information Technology Infrastructure Library (ITIL) that includes a CCB for command-owned information systems. Additionally, ensure the local configurations are consistent with command configurations. (It is a command responsibility to update the Configuration Management Database (CMDB) and ensure that the Enterprise Configuration Control Board (ECCB) is aware of any system or network issues).

13. Ensure that all information technology users are appropriately trained on the legitimate and authorized use of systems, have signed user agreements, and have a valid need to access Marine Corps IT systems.

14. Ensure that only validated materiel solutions are acquired in support of defined capabilities compliant with DoD, DON, and Marine Corps cybersecurity policy and guidance applicable to the particular materiel solutions.

(i) Marine Corps Information Systems Security Managers (ISSM) shall:

1. Note that the term "ISSM" replaced "IAM".

2. Establish and manage the cybersecurity program within a command, site, system, or enclave in accordance with DoD, DON, and Marine Corps cybersecurity guidance and policies.

3. Manage the command, site, system, or enclave C&A process to ensure that information systems within their purview are approved, operated, and maintained throughout its life cycle in accordance with the information system's accreditation package.

     4. Serve as the principal advisor to the commander for site, system, or enclave cybersecurity matters on behalf of the AO.

     5. Assess the cybersecurity program effectiveness and mitigate efficiencies in accordance with the references.

     6. Ensure information systems are compliant with the IAVM Program (i.e., IAVAs, and IAVBs) and all applicable Security Technical Implementation Guide (STIG) in addition to accurate compliance information reporting in accordance with references (a) and (w).

     7. Ensure cybersecurity workforce personnel receive required security training commensurate with their security duties in accordance with reference (x).

     8. Report all issues/concerns regarding POR, CMP, and UUNS to the appropriate MARCORSYSCOM program offices, MCNOSC Vulnerability Management Team (VMT), or DC CD&I CDD integration division for resolution.

     9. Ensure that security incidents (e.g., malicious code, attacks, intrusions, violations, spillages, etc.) are reported to the MARCERT in a timely manner in accordance with references (w) and (y).

     10. Ensure MARCERT directed protective/corrective actions are implemented for security incident remediation or mitigation.

     11. Serve as an active member of CCBs to affect control and security management of all information systems, devices, configurations, and cybersecurity implementations within their purview.

     (j) <u>Marine Corps Information Systems Security Officers (ISSO) shall</u>:

     1. Note that the term "ISSO" replaced "IAO".

2. Report to the ISSM and ensure an appropriate cybersecurity posture is maintained for a command, site, system, or enclave.

3. Provide direct support to the ISSM for all cybersecurity matters.

4. Assist the ISSM in updating, creating, and reviewing accreditation packages.

5. Enforce system-level IA controls in accordance with the proper program and policy guidance.

6. Evaluate risks, threats, and vulnerabilities to determine if additional safeguards are needed to protect the command, site, system, or enclave.

7. Ensure that all information systems and networks within their purview are planned, installed, operated, maintained, managed, and accredited within the security requirements of the information system or network.

8. Develop and issue any additional specific cybersecurity policies, guidance, and instructions as needed.

9. Assist the ISSM in monitoring, reporting, and enforcing the Command, site, system, or enclave IAVM program.

(k) Marine Corps System and Network Administrators (SYSADMIN/NTWKADMIN) shall:

1. Monitor user account activity and establish procedures for investigating, deactivating, and deleting accounts that do not show activity over time.

2. Provide cybersecurity safeguards and assurances to the data under their control as well as their personal authentication and authorization mechanisms.

3. Analyze patterns of non-compliance or unauthorized activity and take appropriate administrative or programmatic actions to minimize security risks and insider threats.

<u>4</u>. Recognize potential security violations, take appropriate action to report the incident as required by regulation, and remediate or mitigate any adverse impact.

<u>5</u>. Implement applicable patches, including IAVAs and IAVBs and critical security updates in a timely manner to avoid potential compromise or loss of functionality.

<u>6</u>. Manage accounts, network rights, and access to information systems and equipment.

<u>7</u>. Configure, optimize, and test hosts (e.g., servers and workstations) and network devices (e.g., hubs, routers, and switches) to ensure compliance with security policy, procedures, and technical requirements.

<u>8</u>. Install, test, maintain, and upgrade operating systems, software, and hardware to comply with prescribed cybersecurity requirements.

<u>9</u>. Ensure that hardware, software, data, and facility resources are archived, sanitized, or disposed of in a manner compliant with system security plans, requirements, and regulations.

<u>10</u>. Perform audit log review on network, systems and applications in accordance with the applicable STIGs.

(1) <u>MCEN Information Systems Users shall</u>:

<u>1</u>. A user is defined as any military, government civilian, or contractor who has authorized access to the GIG or Marine Corps IT resources.

<u>2</u>. Obtain a favorable background investigation and hold a security clearance or access approvals commensurate with the level of information processed or available on the system.

<u>3</u>. Comply with this Order and other cybersecurity directives, policies, and guidance as established by higher headquarters. Supplemental cybersecurity guidance, updates, or revisions will be provided through Enterprise Information Assurance Directives (EIADs)/Enterprise

Cybersecurity Directives (ECSDs), Marine Administration (MARADMIN) messages, and Marine Corps Bulletins (MCBUL).

   4. Comply with the guidelines established in accordance with reference (x) and submit a DD 2875 System Authorization Access Request (SAAR) along with an Acceptable Use Agreement when using Government-owned information systems.

   5. Receive cybersecurity indoctrination training and attend annual cybersecurity refresher training in accordance with reference (x).

   6. Mark, label, and safeguard all media, devices, peripherals, and information systems at the security level for which they are intended and in accordance with DoD, DON, and Marine Corps policies and procedures. Dissemination shall only be made to individuals with a need to know and clearance level at or above the classification level of the shared media, device, or peripheral.

   7. Protect all media, devices, peripherals, and information systems located in their respective area of responsibility in accordance with physical security and data protection requirements.

   8. Practice safe Intranet and Internet operating principles and take no actions that threaten the integrity of the system or network in accordance with this Order.

   9. Report incidents or suspicious events regarding suspected intrusions or unauthorized access; circumvention of security procedures; presence of suspicious files or programs; receipt of suspicious email attachments, files, or links; spillage incidents; and malicious logic (e.g. viruses, trojan horses, worms, spamming, phishing, chain letters, etc.) to the ISSM, ISSO, or SYSADMIN.

   10. Report the receipt or discovery of unfamiliar or unauthorized removable media (e.g., CD-ROM, floppy disk, thumb drives, external hard drives, etc.) to the ISSM, SYSADMIN, or NTWKADMIN in accordance with applicable directives.

   11. Use anti-virus (AV) products on all files, attachments, and media before opening or introducing them into the information system.

12. Report suspicious, erratic, or anomalous information systems operations; missing or added files; and non-approved services or programs to the SYSADMIN or NTWKADMIN in accordance with local policy and cease operations on the affected information system until authorized to start operations again by higher authority.

13. Comply with cryptographic log-in requirements and password or pass-phrase policy directives, and protect information systems from unauthorized access.

14. Logoff and secure the information system and work environment (e.g., secure For Official Use Only [FOUO] media, remove Common Access Card (CAC), etc.) at the end of each workday or when out of the immediate area.

15. Access only data, controlled information, software, hardware, and firmware for which they are authorized access and have a need to know. Assume only authorized roles and privileges.

16. Government-provided and installed cybersecurity products (e.g., anti-virus, virtual private networks [VPNs], personal firewalls, etc.) will not be altered, circumvented, or disabled on Marine Corps information systems.

17. Authorized Government-provided cybersecurity products (e.g., AV, VPNs, personal firewalls, etc.) are encouraged to be installed and updated on personal systems as required by the AO for approved remote access.

18. Prohibited activities. The following activities are specifically prohibited and users will not:

(a) Use official Government information systems for commercial gain or conduct illegal activities.

(b) Use information systems in any manner that interferes with official duties, undermines readiness, reflects adversely on the Marine Corps, or violates standards of ethical conduct.

(c) Intentionally send, store, or propagate sexually explicit, threatening, harassing, prohibited partisan political, or unofficial public (e.g., "spam") communications.

(d) Participate in on-line gambling or other activities inconsistent with public service.

(e) Participate in, install, configure, or use unauthorized peer-to-peer (P2P) technologies.

(f) Release, disclose, or alter information without the consent of the data owner, the original classification authority (OCA), the individual's supervisory chain of command, Freedom of Information Act (FOIA) official, Public Affairs Officer (PAO), or the disclosure officer's approval.

(g) Attempt to strain, test, circumvent, or bypass security mechanisms; perform network line monitoring; or keystroke monitoring.

(h) Modify system or software, use it in any manner other than its intended purpose, introduce malicious software or code, or add user-configurable or unauthorized software (e.g., unauthorized instant messaging, P2P applications).

(i) Relocate or change information system equipment or information system equipment network connectivity without proper security authorization.

(j) Share personal accounts and passwords or allow remote access to non-privileged users.

(k) Disable or remove security or protective software or mechanisms.

(l) Acquire commercial or unauthorized internet service provider (ISP) network access into Marine Corps operational facilities without approval from the Marine Corps AO.

(m) Implement commercial wireless components (e.g., access points, base stations, clients, etc.) without approval from the Marine Corps AO.

(n) Use wireless technologies for storing, processing, and transmitting unclassified information in areas where classified information is discussed, stored, processed, or transmitted without the express written consent of the Marine Corps AO.

(o) Auto forward email from government accounts to commercial ISP email services; engage in the creation or forwarding chain mail; or open email attachments or internet links received from unknown sources.

(m) Coordinating Instructions

1. Military users in violation of DoD, DON, and Marine Corps cybersecurity policies and procedures may be subject to disciplinary actions under the Uniform Code of Military Justice (UCMJ), Federal, or State criminal statutes and laws.

2. Violation of this Order by government or contractor civilian personnel may result in personnel actions under 5 CFR 2635.101(b)(9) and (14), the Federal Acquisition Regulation (FAR), or referral of criminal violations to appropriate civilian authorities.

3. Establish a comprehensive program to implement, document, and manage a standard Configuration Management Program (CMP) across the MCEN for all non POR systems.

4. Ensure Marine Corps networks are Public Key-enabled in accordance with reference (ak) and USCYBERCOM directives.

5. Administration and Logistics

a. This Order shall not alter or supersede existing authoritative policies issued by the ODNI regarding the protection of SCI and special access programs (SAPs) for intelligence. The application of the provisions and procedures of this Order to SCI or other intelligence information systems is encouraged where they may complement or address areas not otherwise specifically identified.

b. Detailed cybersecurity practices and procedures supporting the MCCSP will be published and released by HQMC C4, or HQMC I/SEO.

c. Recommendations for changes to this Order should be submitted to HQMC C4 via the appropriate chain of command.

d. All developers, owners, and users of information systems and applications within MCEN have the responsibility to establish and implement adequate operation and information technology controls including records management requirements to ensure the proper maintenance and use of records, regardless of format or medium, to promote accessibility and authorized retention per the approved records schedule and reference (ah).

e. Further restrictions to any parts of this Order require the express permission of the Marine Corps AO.

f. Records created as a result of this Order shall be managed according to National Archives and Records Administration approved dispositions per reference (am) to ensure porper maintenance, use, accessibility and preservation, regardless of format or medium.

6. Command and Signal

a. Command. This Order is applicable to the Marine Corps to include Marine Corps Reserves and any personnel employed by or in support of Marine Corps Total Force System.

b. Signal. This Order is effective the date signed.

KEVIN J. NALLY
Director, Command, Control,
Communications, and Computers

DISTRIBUTION: PCN 10207719100

DEFINITIONS

Authorizing Official (AO) - The Authorizing Official is a senior official or executive with the authority to formally assume responsibility for operating in information system at an acceptable level of risk to organizational operations and assets, individuals, other organizations, and Nation. Authorizing officials typically have budgetary oversight for an information system or are responsible for the mission and/or business operations supported by the system. Through the security authorization process, authorizing officials are accountable for security risks associated with information system operations. Accordingly, authorizing officials are in management positions with a level of authority commensurate with understanding and accepting such information system-related security risks. Authorizing officials also approve security plans, memorandums of agreement or understanding, and plans of action and milestones and determine whether significant changes in the information systems or environments of operation system or if the system is operational, halt operations, if unacceptable risks exist. Authorizing officials coordinate their activities with the risk executive (function), chief information officer, senior information security officer, common control providers, and other interested parties during the security authorization process. With the increasing complexity of mission/business processes, partnership arrangements, and the use of external/shared services, it is possible that a particular information system may involve multiple authorizing officials. If so, agreements are established among the authorizing officials and documented in the security plan. Authorizing officials are responsible for ensuring that all activities and functions associated with security authorization that are delegated to authorizing officials designated representatives are carried out. The role of authorizing official has inherent U.S. Government authority and is assigned to government personnel only. This term has replaced Designated Accrediting Authority (DAA). (REF CNSSI 4009)

Configuration Control Board (CCB) - The purpose of the CCB is to ensure each proposed change to an item's performance or physical characteristics is thoroughly evaluated with respect to technical, logistics, cost, and schedule impacts and benefits. Review and input by the CCB allows the approval authority to make sound, informed management decisions. (REF CNSSI 4009)

Configuration Management Database (CMDB) — A database that contains relevant details (e.g., settings, firmware revisions, etc.) of Configuration Items (CIs) and the relationships between them. For example, information about a network switch might include the software release installed on it, and the servers that connect directly to it, all of which would also be CIs. (REF ITIL Version 2.0)

Configuration Management Program (CMP) - Applies appropriate processes and tools to establish and maintain consistency between the product and the product requirements and attributes defined in product configuration information. Configuration Management shall be applicable to all hardware, software, and firmware items and associated documents. A disciplined CM process ensures that products conform to their requirements and are identified and documented in sufficient detail to support the product life cycle. (Defense Acquisition Guidebook)

Cyberspace domain - A global domain within the information environment consisting of the interdependent network of information technology infrastructures, including the internet, telecommunications networks, computer systems, and imbedded processors and controllers. (REF CNSSI 4009 and NIST IR 7298.)

Cybersecurity - Protection of data and information systems in networks that connect to other networks or the Internet. This is done by means of preventing, detecting, and responding to attacks. (REF CNSSI 4009)

Cybersecurity Steering Group (CSSG) - Established under the C4 OAG to facilitate the timely formulation of security solutions to meet current and future force objectives. The CSSG will address, mitigate, and validate security issues in order to protect the Marine Corps to an acceptable level. Core members of the CSSG include HQMC C4, MARCORSYSCOM, MARFORCYBER, DC CD&I, Marine Corps Operational Test and Evaluation Activity (MCOTEA), Marine Corps Training and Education Command (TECOM), Marine Corps Intelligence Activity (MCIA), and Marine Corps Community Services (MCCS).

Enterprise Configuration Control Board (ECCB) - The ECCB exists to approve or otherwise act on Requests for Change (RFC) to established or nominated configuration items that operate within the MCEN. RFCs may contain a range of capabilities from minor changes to major system projects. It will be the concern of the ECCB to enforce good practices, enforce DoD, DON, and Marine Corps standards and accepted industry methodologies when considering configuration changes.

Identity Assurance - The capability to affix, verify, and/or determine the identity of a person (living, deceased, unconscious, non-functioning, uncooperative, or unaware), an organization, or other entity. Identity Assurance can facilitate intelligence collection, targeting, combat identification, and analysis on individuals, groups, and their activities. It can also be referenced as part of Supply Chain Protection. (REF NIST SP 800-63.)

Information Systems - These include, but are not limited to, computers, processors, devices, or environments (operating in a prototype, test bed, training, stand-alone, integrated, embedded, or networked configuration) that receive, process, store, display, or transmit government or government supporting information, regardless of mission assurance category, sensitivity or classification, with or without handling codes and caveats. This includes information systems used for teleworking and telecommuting; contractor owned or operated information systems residing on the Marine Corps Enterprise Network (MCEN); information systems obtained with Non-Appropriated Funds; Urgent Universal Need Statements (UUNS), automated tactical systems (ATSs); automated weapons systems (AWSs); platform information technology (PIT); and distributed computing environments (DCEs). Systems processing intelligence information are required to adhere to the provisions of this Order. (REF CNSSI 4009)

Information Systems Security Manager (ISSM) - The roles and responsibilities of the Information Systems Security Manager, as referenced in this document, are aligned to the roles and responsibilities of the DoD 8500.1 and DoDI 8510.01 Information Assurance Manager and the CJCSI 6510.01F Information Systems Security Manager. This term has replaced IAM. (REF CNSSI 4009)

Information Systems Security Officer (ISSO) - The roles and responsibilities of the Information Systems Security Officer, as referenced in this document, are aligned to the roles and responsibilities of the DoDI 8500.2 Information Assurance Officer and the CJCSI 6510.01F Information Systems Security Officer. This term has replaced IAO. (REF CNSSI 4009)

Marine Corps Certification and Accreditation Process (MCCAP) - Marine Corps Enterprise Information Assurance Directive 018, 2 September 2008, established the MCCAP to provide a comprehensive and uniform approach to the certification and accreditation process for the Marine Corps, to include all subordinate commands, bases, and organizations.

Marine Corps Enterprise Network (MCEN) -The Marine Corps' network-of-networks and approved interconnected network segments. It comprises people, processes, logical and physical infrastructure, architecture, topology, and Cyberspace Operations.

Marine Corps Intelligence, Surveillance, Reconnaissance – Enterprise (MCISR-E) – The MCISR-E is a framework to develop an ISR enterprise to meet the specified and implied tasks identified in the Marine Corps Service Campaign Plan.

Marine Corps Sensitive Compartmented Intelligence (SCI) Enterprise Office (SEO) - The SEO administers and operates the Marine Corps SCI Enterprise by providing policy implementation, governance, technical support, and assistance in establishing and sustaining Marine Corps SCI activities. The SEO coordinates strategic and enterprise initiatives in support of MCISR-E to meet operational requirement for Distributed Operations, Net-Centric Operations, Interoperability, Enterprise Architectures, Service-oriented Architecture, and Information Management. The SEO provides Enterprise Management, Network Operations, Network Security, Information Assurance and Asset Management across the Marine Corps in accordance with relevant directives and guidance from the ODNI, Department of Defense Intelligence Information Systems (DODIIS), Defense Intelligence Agency (DIA), and National Security Agency (NSA).

Marine Corps Web Risk Assessment Cell (MCWRAC) - The MCWRAC conducts Web Risk Assessments (WRAs) of Marine Corps organizational web sites to identify Operations Security (OPSEC) and Cybersecurity vulnerabilities, issues, and/or concerns. The MCWRAC mission is to ensure that publicly accessible, non-restricted, Marine Corps World Wide Web (WWW) sites are protected against malicious activities intended to deny, degrade, or disrupt public access to Marine Corps web sites or modify the content in any way.

Point of Presence (POP) - A demarcation point or interface point between network or communications entities. (REF CJCSI 6211.02D.)

Vulnerability Management Team (VMT) – The primary reporting agent within the MCNOSC designated to manage the Marine Corps vulnerability management programming support of the USCYBERCOM and DoD IAVM program. The VMT is responsible to maintain access and administration of the Marine Corps Vulnerability Management System (VMS) and ensure dissemination or availability of IAVM notifications for personnel responsible for implementing and managing responses to information system vulnerabilities.

ACRONYMS

AO	Authorizing Official
AV	Anti-Virus
C4	Command, Control, Communications, and Computers
C&A	Certification and Accreditation
CAC	Common Access Card
CCB	Configuration Control Board
CD&I	Combat Development and Integration
CDS	Cross Domain Solution
CI	Counter Intelligence
CIO	Chief Information Officer
CMC	Commandant of the Marine Corps
CMDB	Configuration Management Database
CMP	Configuration Management Program
CND	Computer Network Defense
CNO	Computer Network Operations
CNSS	Committee on National Security Systems
COCOM	Combatant Command
COMSEC	Communication Security
COTS	Commercial Off the Shelf
CSSG	Cybersecurity Steering Group
CYBERCON	Cybersecurity Condition
DAA	Designated Accrediting Authority
DC PP&O	Deputy Commandant Plans, Policy, and Operations
DCO	Defensive Cyber Operations
DGO	DoD Gig Operations
DIA	Defense Intelligence Agency
DIACAP	DOD Information Assurance Certification and Accreditation Process
DIRINT	Director of Intelligence
DISN	Defense Information Systems Network
DITPR-DON	Department of Defense Information Technology Portfolio Repository Department of the Navy
DITS	Digital Integrated Transport Suites
DoD	Department of Defense
DON	Department of the Navy
DOTMLPF	Doctrine, Organization, Training, Materiel, Leadership and Education, Personnel, Facilities
DR/COOP	Disaster Recovery/Continuity of Operations Plan
DSAWG	Defense/Information Assurance Security Accreditation Working Group
ECCB	Enterprise Configuration Control Board
ECSD	Enterprise Cybersecurity Directive
EIAD	Enterprise Information Assurance Directive
EKMS	Electronic Key Management System

ESSG	Enterprise-wide Information Assurance and Computer Network Defense Solutions Steering Group
FAR	Federal Acquisition Regulation
FISMA	Federal Information Security Management Act
FOIA	Freedom of Information Act
FOUO	For Official Use Only
GIG	Global Information Grid
GOTS	Government Off the Shelf
IA	Information Assurance
IASG	Information Assurance Steering Group
IAVA	Information Assurance Vulnerability Alert
IAVB	Information Assurance Vulnerability Bulletin
IAVM	Information Assurance Vulnerability Management
IDS	Intrusion Detection System
IGMC	Inspector General of the Marine Corps
IO	Information Operations
IPS	Intrusion Prevention System
ISP	Internet Service Provider
IT	Information Technology
ITIL	Information Technology Infrastructure Library
JCIDS	Joint Capabilities Integration Development Systems
JKMIWG	Joint Key Management Infrastructure Working Group
KMEC	Key Management Executive Committee
KMI	Key Management Infrastructure
LE	Law enforcement
MAIS	Major Automated Information System
MARADMIN	Marine Corps Administrative Messages
MARCERT	Marine Corps Computer Emergency Response Team
MARFOR	Marine Forces
MARFORCYBER	Marine Corps Forces Cyber Command
MARCORSYSCOM	Marine Corps Systems Command
MCBUL	Marine Corps Bulletin
MCCAP	Marine Corps Certification and Accreditation Process
MCCAT	Marine Corps Cyber Assessment Team
MCCSP	Marine Corps Cybersecurity Program
MCEN	Marine Corps Enterprise Network
MCISR-E	Marine Corps Intelligence, Surveillance, Reconnaissance - Enterprise.
MCNOSC	Marine Corps Network and Operations Security Center
MDAPS	Mandatory Procedures for Major Defense Acquisition Programs
MDID	Market-Driven/Industry-Developed
MOS	Military Occupational Specialty

MWRAC	Marine Corps Web Risk Assessment Cell
NAS	Naval Audit Service
NCIS	Naval Criminal Investigative Service
NCMS	Naval Communications Security Management Service
NETOPS	Network Operations
NIST	National Institute of Standards and Technology
NTWKADMIN	Network Administrator
NSA	National Security Agency
OAG	Operational Advisory Group
OCA	Original Classification Authority
ODNI	Office of the Director of National Intelligence
OCO	Offensive Cyber Operations
OPSEC	Operations Security
P2P	Peer to Peer
PAO	Public Affairs Officer
PII	Personally Identifiable Information
PKI	Public Key Infrastructure
POA&M	Plan of Action and Milestones
POM	Program Objective Memorandum
POP	Point of Presence
POR	Program of Record
PM	Program Manager
RDT&E	Research, Development, Test, and Evaluation
SAP	Special Access Program
SCI	Sensitive Compartmented Information
SCIF	Sensitive Compartmented Information Facility
SEO	Sensitive Compartmented Information (SCI) Enterprise Office
SIAO	Senior Information Assurance Official
SISS	Subcommittee for Information Systems Security
STIG	Security Technical Information Guidelines
ST&E	Security, Test, and Evaluation
STS	Subcommittee for Telecommunications Security
SYSADMIN	Systems Administrator
T&R	Training and Readiness
TTP	Tactics, Techniques, and Procedures
UCMJ	Uniform Code of Military Justice
USCYBERCOM	United States Cyber Command
UUNS	Urgent Universal Needs Statement
VMT	Vulnerability Management Team
VPN	Virtual Private Network